Activities for Mentoring Young People

Activities for Mentoring Young People

Stephanie George

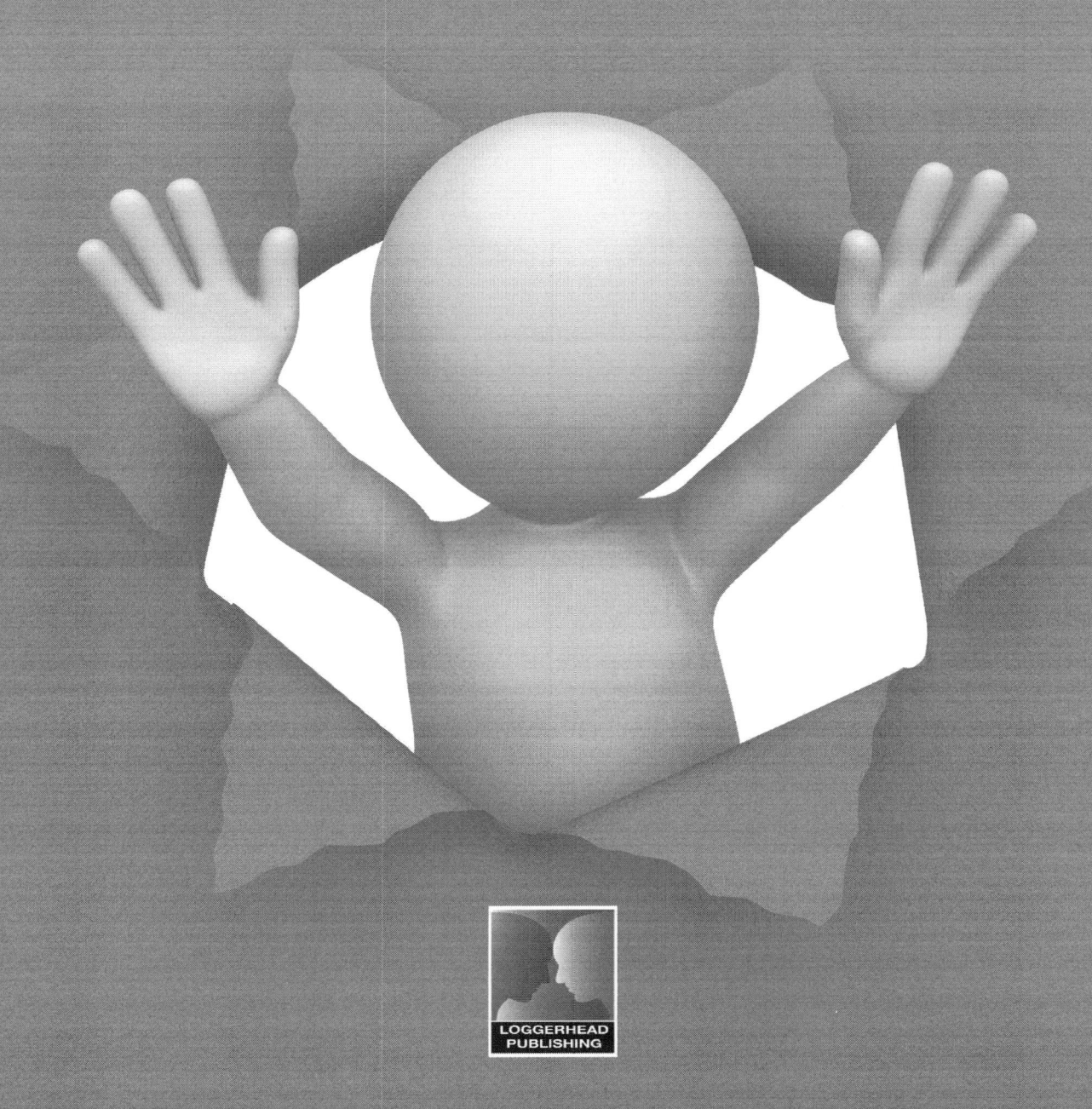

LOGGERHEAD PUBLISHING

First published in 2013 by

Loggerhead Publishing Ltd, PO Box 928, Northampton NN7 9AP, United Kingdom
Tel: 0845 605 0230 International Tel: +44 203 239 3432
Fax: 0808 280 0937 International Fax: +44 1280 850 718

www.loggerheadpublishing.co.uk

© S George 2013

All rights reserved. The whole of this work including all text and illustrations is protected by copyright. No part of it may be copied, altered, adapted or otherwise exploited in any way without express prior permission, unless in accordance with the provisions of the Copyright Designs and Patents Act 1988 or in order to photocopy or make duplicating masters of those pages so indicated, without alteration and including all copyright notices, for the express purpose of instruction. No parts of this work may otherwise be loaded, stored, manipulated, reproduced or transmitted in any form or by any means, electronic or mechanical, including photocopying and recording, or by any information storage and retrieval system, without prior written permission from the publisher, on behalf of the copyright owner.

Printed in the United Kingdom.

Designed by Moo Creative (Luton)

British Library Cataloguing in Publication Data. A catalogue record for this book is available from the British Library

ISBN 978-1-909380-03-5

Contents

About the author vi

Acknowledgements vii

Introduction viii

How to use this book x

Activities

    Knowing Me, Knowing You   1

    Planning the Journey   3

    Initial Self-Assessment   9

    Student Re-Assessment and Evaluation   11

    Target Setting and Action Planning   15

    Review – Target Setting and Action Planning   19

    Show Me the Difference   21

    Improving Attendance   24

    And the Moral of the Story is …   29

    Let Me Tell You a Story   34

    What if?   38

    The Treasure Hunt   41

    Sunshine Thinking   48

    I Remember When … It Happened to Me   51

    Oh No! Sarah's in Trouble   54

    Conflict – What it is and How to Deal with it   58

    I'm Seeing Red   64

    Stop Seeing Red   69

    It's About Time   72

    A Place to Study   78

About the author

Stephanie George is a teacher, trainer and author of *The Learning Mentor Manual* (Sage, 2010), the leading educational textbook on mentor practice in England. She has experience of working with teams of mentors in a variety of challenging settings. Stephanie has been responsible for the training and development of Learning Mentors since their inception and regularly runs courses and INSET on all aspects of mentoring practice in schools. She is also the recipient of two Department for Education Excellence in Cities awards.

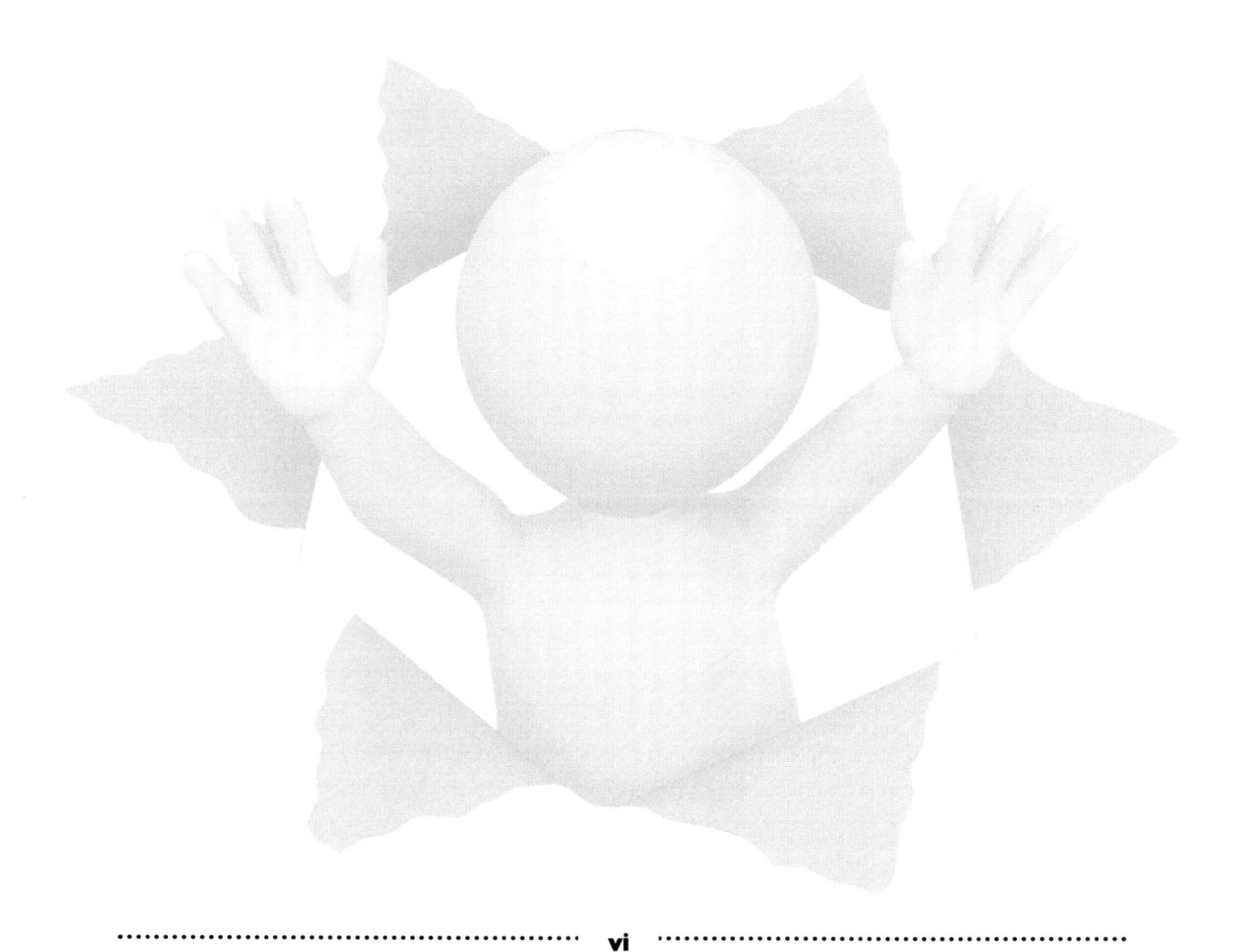

Acknowledgements

I would not have completed this book if it was not for the dedicated help of Jeba Begum, a talented English graduate and Educational Mentor, who helped with typing up the manuscript and proofreading.

Thank you to Patricia St Louis who continues to promote quality Mentoring practice in our corner of London. I am grateful to her for listening patiently to my creative, if sometimes unorthodox, ideas.

Thank you to Sue Christelow for all of her help with editing and final preparations. Thank you to Catherine McAllister, my publisher, for her faith in me.

To Jackie, Joanie and Jennie, I am fortunate to have you as my sisters.

To Gracie and Josh for their patience.

Thank you to my parents.

Introduction

The idea for this book was inspired directly by Learning Mentors, pastoral leaders, youth workers, house leaders and those in similar pastoral roles that I have met up and down the UK over the last three years in Birmingham, Leeds, Liverpool , Manchester, Leicester and London, who have asked me about appropriate resources for mentoring. This book is for them.

The activities aim to provide specific structured tasks that can be used during mentoring meetings and support mentoring intervention by:

1. Offering issue-specific activities, e.g. the activity 'I'm Seeing Red'.

2. Provide structure for building rapport, e.g. the anger-issue activity 'Knowing Me, Knowing You'.

3. Give opportunities for written evidence of progress for the student, e.g. the student self-assessment and reassessment activities.

Within this book there are 20 mentoring-specific activities that cross the bridge between the pastoral and curriculum aspects of learning – the best practice tells us that one without the other does not serve the needs of our young people well. That really is the point; education, after all, is about the whole child, the quality of teaching and appropriate intervention to support the achievement of young people.

Getting it right should be about relentless pursuit. I use the analogy of baking a cake; it seems that everyone I know likes cake. So, first of all, we need the right ingredients: flour, eggs, sugar and butter, and with baking, measurements must be precise. Now without raising agent the cake is flat, without sugar the cake is tasteless and without eggs, we actually have biscuits, nice, but not what we intended. Then we add cooking time, appropriate temperature and check the oven frequently.

Achieving academic and social success for the young people in our care is somewhat similar: we must have the right ingredients and method, and an eye for precision. Consider this recipe:

- An appropriate and suitable curriculum for your cohort

- Intervention as necessary to address the needs of the student

- Delivered in a timely fashion, suitable for the cohort

- High-quality teaching

- Frequent and thorough monitoring of progress

- Finally, support the student in all areas, social, academic, emotional and physically to nurture and enhance achievement.

The resources and activities in this book aim to help you to help the young people that you are working with by ultimately focusing upon one thing – their achievement.

How to use this book

The objective of this book is to give Mentors a range of resources that can be used during mentoring intervention. Each activity is mapped specifically against Ofsted Spiritual Moral Social and Cultural (SMSC) Development criteria (Ofsted Evaluation Framework September 2012 onwards), and the SMSC criteria applicable are indicated.

In addition many of the activities resonate with Ofsted criteria in terms of the quality of teaching and learning and behaviour, particularly with regard to the following:

- Addressing students' attitudes to learning
- Addressing students' attendance and punctuality at school and in lessons
- Considering students' progress relative to their starting points
- Addressing students' communication skills
- Encouraging consistently high expectations of students
- Improving the quality of learning effectively by checking students' understanding across the curriculum and making appropriate interventions
- Giving constructive feedback so as to contribute to students' learning

My aim is that the activities assist with demonstrating progress of mentoring intervention in a concrete way.

The activities are framed as follows:

1. Activity Objective
2. Intended Audience
3. SMSC Criteria/Ofsted Criteria
4. Context
5. Activity Instructions
6. Closing the Activity

All of the activities have accompanying activity sheets, which are numbered. Most of the activities can be used discretely as standalone activities. However, one or two run consecutively e.g. baseline assessment and subsequent reassessment. Any activity can be selected to address a particular need with a student.

At the very heart of this book is a set of activities that enable Mentors to demonstrate the impact of mentoring intervention.

Most importantly the activities, once complete, will provide you with evidence of work with students that is demonstrable to them and other stakeholders.

Activity

Knowing Me, Knowing You

Activity Objective
To provide an opportunity to build rapid rapport with a student.

Intended Audience
Individual

Spiritual, Moral, Social and Cultural Development Criteria
- Understanding the consequences of their actions.
- Sense of enjoyment and fascination in learning about themselves, others and the world around them, including the intangible.
- Beliefs, religious or otherwise, which inform their perspective on life and their interest in and respect for different people's feelings and values.

Context
The first few meetings with the students that you are mentoring may be challenging, particularly if they are unsure of the reasons for your intervention.
The suggestion here for breaking the ice, so to speak, is to get the student to flip the script. Let the student interview you!
- Why? The pressure is immediately taken off the student.
- Why? For some students, the sense of empowerment this gives them is too enticing to resist. (You, however, are always in control as the supportive adult – your responses can be fanciful.)
- Why? This activity is fun and takes the student by surprise.
- Why? It conveys that you, an adult in the school, are willing to trust them. This alone will save you weeks of time.

Activity Instructions
1. You prepare the questionnaire in advance so you decide what you want to be asked. A sample questionnaire is provided in Activity Sheet 1.
2. A few simple questions that take the tension out of the meeting and you are likely to find the student much more willing to engage next time you meet.
3. Now that the student has had an opportunity to ask the questions, reverse the activity and ask the student some questions. Use the same ones and observe what happens.

Closing the Activity
Students just love this activity. It demonstrates to them that you are willing to trust them and therein begins a very powerful aspect of building rapport. In turn this should yield benefits in terms of creating quality mentoring conversations.

Activities for Mentoring Young People

1 Activity Sheet

Knowing Me, Knowing You Questions

1. What is your favourite food?

2. What is/was your favourite subject at school? Tell me more about how it came to be so.

3. If your house was flooded and you had to save something what would it be? Tell me more about that choice.

4. If you had a choice between hot and cold, which would you choose and why?

5. If you had a choice between a train or a bus, which would you prefer? Tell me more about that choice.

6. If you had a choice between being beautiful or rich, which would you choose? Tell me more about that choice.

7. If you had a choice of a hot-air balloon or a kite what would you choose? Tell me more about that choice.

8. Who is the bravest person you know? Tell me more about them.

9. If you had a choice between music or television which would you prefer? Tell me more about that choice.

10. If you had a choice between shoes or slippers which would you prefer? Tell me more about that choice.

Activity

Planning the Journey

Activity Objective
To give students the opportunity to assess a baseline for improvement.

Intended Audience
Individual

Spiritual, Moral, Social and Cultural Development Criteria
- Willingness to reflect on their experiences.

Context
As is the case with any journey before we leave home, it is best to know where we are going, so we plan a route. To plan the most efficient route we look at a starting point and destination. This activity is about discovering where we will start and the direction that we need to move in.

Activity Instructions
1. The student begins by completing the questionnaire on Activity Sheet 2.
2. Activity Sheet 3 is then used to calculate scores and provide a Diagnostic Assessment of the responses. The assessment sheets are subdivided into three categories: A, B and C. Each category assessment provides key questions for discussion following the assessment. The key questions provide an opportunity to drill down and identify areas to look at in mentoring.

Closing the Activity
This activity will provide a wealth of information. From this you will be able to prepare an action plan for the journey forward.
See the activity entitled 'Target Setting and Action Planning'.

Activities for Mentoring Young People

2 Activity Sheet

Planning the Journey Assessment

Assessing the start of your journey

		YES	NO	MAYBE
1.	My school work and social life are balanced	☐	☐	☐
2.	I have ample time to do all of the things I want to do (socially and school related)	☐	☐	☐
3.	I like my peer group and friends and they are supportive	☐	☐	☐
4.	I am able to resolve disputes with my friends amicably	☐	☐	☐
5.	My family supports me with my school work and studies	☐	☐	☐
6.	I have a regular routine for evenings during term time	☐	☐	☐
7.	I participate in extra-curriculum activities at school	☐	☐	☐
8.	I get enough sleep and rest, and eat a balanced diet at home	☐	☐	☐
9.	I have met homework and coursework deadlines	☐	☐	☐
10.	I am confident about my future and have begun to make plans for when I leave school	☐	☐	☐

© Stephanie George. May be reproduced for instructional use only

3 Activity Sheet

Assessment Scoring

Responses	Score
2 points – YES	
1 point – MAYBE	
0 point – NO	

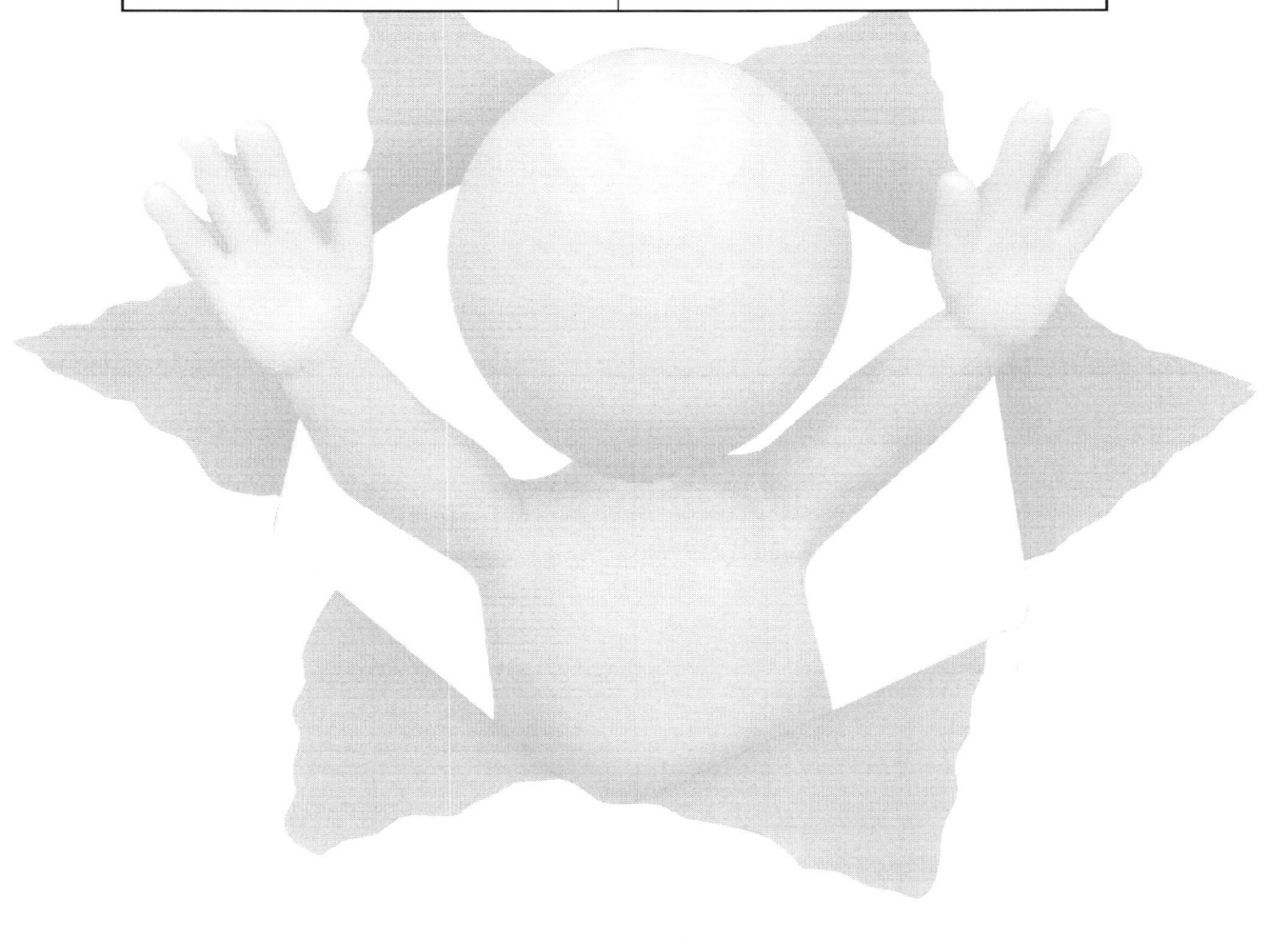

Activities for Mentoring Young People

3a Activity Sheet

Diagnostic Scoring Summary

Category A
16 – 20 points

A. Wow! You are clearly on your way to achieving your potential.

You have an idea of the direction you wish to take and have already identified some of the elements that contribute to your success. This includes regular routines, a structured approach to homework, coursework and social skills that enable you to negotiate disputes or management of conflicts with confidence.

What you need to do now:

You need to plan with your mentor how to maximise your achievement.

Key questions:

- What do you do well?

- What skills do you use when you achieve success?

- Can these skills be used in other areas or subjects?

3b Activity Sheet

Diagnostic Scoring Summary

Category B
11 – 15 points

B. Fantastic! You are on the road to maximising all opportunities of achievement.

There may be times when you find some situations difficult to manage. Your scores reveal that you may need support, guidance and help with organising or planning your work or perhaps there are tensions that interfere with you taking advantage of the opportunities to maximise your potential.

What you need to do now:

You will need to plan with your mentor the journey to reaching your fullest potential.

Key questions:

- How do you use your time for completing homework and coursework?
- Do you have friendships that support or hinder your progress?
- What support is available at home?
- How well do you manage challenging situations?

3c Activity Sheet

Diagnostic Scoring Summary

Category C
0 – 10 points

C. Ok, don't panic! What this is telling us is that we need to get hold of this situation and what you have done by completing this assessment is begun your journey! So well done.

There are several issues standing in the way of you achieving your fullest potential. There are areas of strength that we must build upon to promote your success.

Key questions:

- How can I organise my time more efficiently? Consider a homework plan for each evening or a 'To Do List'.

- Who can help you? Sister, brother, parents, teachers, mentor or friends?

- How do I waste time?

- If I get into disputes with teachers, students or both, what can I do about this?

- What social skills do I need to develop? Do I need a script to use for those times when I find myself in situations of potential conflict?

- Do I have a suitable place to study? How can this be arranged or provided?

- Am I getting enough rest, sleep and eating a balanced diet? What part of my routine needs attention?

Activity

Initial Self-Assessment

Activity Objective
To give students the opportunity to assess themselves in order to provide a baseline for measuring progress.

Intended Audience
Individual

Spiritual, Moral, Social and Cultural Development Criteria
- Willingness to reflect on their experiences.
- Sense of enjoyment and fascination in learning about themselves, others and the world around them, including the intangible.

Context
One of the key things here is to obtain the student's opinion on their own progress, and how they feel about where they are at the start of mentoring before going ahead. For this purpose I think a simple self-assessment questionnaire developed for the students in your particular organisation or setting is vital.

Activity Instructions
1. The questionnaire is appealing to students. I find that they enjoy 'rating themselves'. Allow the student time to work through the Initial Self-Assessment form (Activity Sheet 4).
2. Review the form and then use it as a basis for the Target Setting and Action Planning activity.
3. Discuss the responses and calculate the totals on the form then move on to the activity Target Setting and Action Planning.

Closing the Activity
Follow this activity with the activity entitled 'Student Re-Assessment and Evaluation' after a given period of time.

Activities for Mentoring Young People

4 Activity Sheet

Initial Self-Assessment Form

Name of Student	Form
Mentor	Date

Please circle one box which best describes you. 1 is low and 10 is high

		LOW RATING → HIGH RATING									
1.	Poor attendance	1	2	3	4	5	6	7	8	9	10	Excellent attendance
2.	Poor punctuality	1	2	3	4	5	6	7	8	9	10	Excellent punctuality
3.	Unhappy	1	2	3	4	5	6	7	8	9	10	Happy
4.	Often angry	1	2	3	4	5	6	7	8	9	10	Peaceful — slow to become angry
5.	Poor presentation of written work	1	2	3	4	5	6	7	8	9	10	Good presentation of written work
6.	Bully others	1	2	3	4	5	6	7	8	9	10	Never involved in bullying
7.	Issues with keeping friends	1	2	3	4	5	6	7	8	9	10	Popular, have lots of friends
8.	Poor attitude to learning	1	2	3	4	5	6	7	8	9	10	Positive attitude to learning
9.	Homework often not complete	1	2	3	4	5	6	7	8	9	10	Homework always complete
10.	Un-cooperative	1	2	3	4	5	6	7	8	9	10	Very cooperative
11.	Behaviour causing concern	1	2	3	4	5	6	7	8	9	10	Excellent behaviour
	Totals — Add up all the scores											OUT OF 110

Student Re-Assessment and Evaluation

Activity Objective

To give students the opportunity to re-assess themselves in order to provide a baseline for measuring progress.

Intended Audience

Individual

Spiritual, Moral, Social and Cultural Development Criteria

- Willingness to reflect on their experiences.
- Sense of enjoyment and fascination in learning about themselves, others and the world around them, including the intangible.

Context

This re-assessment activity should be undertaken at the end of or at suitable intervals during the mentoring process. The 'Initial Self-Assessment' activity should always have been completed first. The re-assessment seeks to establish the difference mentoring has made in a data driven and quantifiable way.

Activity Instructions

1. The student completes the Re-Assessment Form (Activity Sheet 5).

The questions will be familiar, having undertaken the original Initial Self-Assessment Form some time previously.

2. Provide the Re-Assessment Form to the student and allow some time to complete it.

3. You will need:

a) The initial Self-Assessment Form (taken from the activity 'Initial Self-Assessment') completed

b) The Re-Assessment Form completed

c) The Assessment Evaluation Form (Activity Sheet 6)

4. You will need to map the responses for each of the forms onto the Assessment Evaluation Form. You will need to calculate the differences (+ or -). Calculate the total responses for each category. What you will then have is the difference for each category as a negative or

a positive improvement. This data is valuable as you are now able to track the impact of mentoring intervention, using qualitative questions in a quantitative way.

Closing the Activity

Review the gains and losses for each area.

Key Questions:

What needs further work?

What is secure?

What needs further consideration?

5 Activity Sheet

Assessment Evaluation Form

Name of Student		Form	
Mentor		Date	

Please circle one box which best describes you. 1 is low and 10 is high

		LOW RATING → HIGH RATING										
1.	Poor attendance	1	2	3	4	5	6	7	8	9	10	Excellent attendance
2.	Poor punctuality	1	2	3	4	5	6	7	8	9	10	Excellent punctuality
3.	Unhappy	1	2	3	4	5	6	7	8	9	10	Happy
4.	Often angry	1	2	3	4	5	6	7	8	9	10	Peaceful – slow to become angry
5.	Poor presentation of written work	1	2	3	4	5	6	7	8	9	10	Good presentation of written work
6.	Bully others	1	2	3	4	5	6	7	8	9	10	Never involved in bullying
7.	Issues with keeping friends	1	2	3	4	5	6	7	8	9	10	Popular, have lots of friends
8.	Poor attitude to learning	1	2	3	4	5	6	7	8	9	10	Positive attitude to learning
9	Homework often not complete	1	2	3	4	5	6	7	8	9	10	Homework always complete
10.	Un-cooperative	1	2	3	4	5	6	7	8	9	10	Very co-operative
11.	Behaviour causing concern	1	2	3	4	5	6	7	8	9	10	Excellent behaviour
	Totals – Add up all the scores											OUT OF 110

Activities for Mentoring Young People

6 Activity Sheet

Mentoring Re-Assessment Form

Name of Student		Form	
Mentor		Date	

		BASELINE RATING (Taken from the initial Assessment Form)	RE-ASSESSMENT RATING (Taken from the Re-Assessment Form)	DIFERRENCE (+/-)
1.	Attendance			
2.	Punctuality			
3.	Happiness			
4.	Often angry			
5.	Presentation of written work			
6.	Bully others			
7.	Issues with keeping friends			
8.	Attitude to learning			
9.	Homework complete			
10.	Co-operation			
11.	Behaviour causing concern			
	Totals – Add up all the scores			

Date of baseline	Baseline Score	Re-Assessment Score	Difference
			+ −

14

© Stephanie George. May be reproduced for instructional use only

Target Setting and Action Planning

Activity Objective
To develop a set of SMART targets and create a plan of action.

Intended Audience
Individual

Spiritual, Moral, Social and Cultural Development Criteria
- Willingness to reflect on their experiences.
- Use of imagination and creativity in their learning.

Context
Best practice in mentoring requires target setting and action planning with the student, as the student needs to plan how they will make progress and what they need to do to get there. The action plan should have SMART features, i.e. it should be Specific, Measurable, Achievable, Realistic and Time focused.

Activity Instructions
1. Stimulate a discussion around target setting with the student – what are the issues that need to be addressed? A focused discussion about the issues affecting learning and achievement needs to take place (use Activity Sheet 7). You and the student then identify the issues affecting learning and achievement. Some aspects to consider during the discussion are:
   a) School report
   b) Grades – current and forecast
   c) Approach to learning and effect
   d) Any marked discrepancies between subjects
   e) Punctuality
   f) Attendance
   g) Relationships with staff
   h) Relationship with peers
   i) Support from home

2. Having had a discussion with the student and developed an area to work on, it is time to set a target and create a plan of action. The plan on Activity Sheet 8 includes the following elements:

a) What does the student wish to achieve?

b) When does the student wish to achieve this?

c) How will the student achieve this?

d) Who will help the student with this?

e) How will the student know that the goal has been achieved? (What evidence will be seen?)

The plan should now be SMART.

Closing the Activity

Review the plan with the student, make any changes to the draft and then finalise the plan. Praise the student to get ready for progress.

Agree a review date, at which you will revisit the plan. See Activity: 'Review – Target Setting and Action Planning'.

7 Activity Sheet

Issues Affecting My Learning and Achievement

Issues affecting my learning and achievement are ...
1.
2.
3.
4.
5.

Activities for Mentoring Young People

8 Activity Sheet

SMART Target Setting and Action Plan

Date | Student Name | Class/Form

What do I want to achieve? (TARGET)	When do I want to achieve it?	How will I achieve my goals?	Who will help me with this?	How will I know I have achieved my goal? (EVIDENCE)
Qualitative Aspect:				
Quantitative Aspect:				

18

© Stephanie George. May be reproduced for instructional use only

Review – Target Setting and Action Planning

Activity Objective
To review a set of targets and prepare a plan of action.

Intended Audience
Individual

Spiritual, Moral, Social and Cultural Development Criteria
- Understanding of the consequences of their actions.
- Willingness to reflect on their experiences.

Context
This activity follows the activity titled 'Target Setting and Action Planning'.

In order for us to know whether an intervention is effective it is crucial that we review any Target Setting and Action Planning that we conduct.

Activity Instructions
You will need the student's original Action Plan. Allow the student to read through and examine this plan. A guided discussion is useful to stimulate thinking. Then using the review grid (Activity Sheet 9), follow the key questions and complete.

Closing the Activity
This activity presents a rich learning opportunity in that it seeks to discover what is the most effective approach based upon the student's prior learning experience and the plan of action that they themselves created.

The evidence gathered from this activity is extremely powerful in that it informs a process for moving forward that is personalised, differentiated and specific to the student's needs.

Celebrate this with the student.

Activities for Mentoring Young People

9 Activity Sheet

Review Grid

	Qualitative Aspect	Quantitative Aspect	What future improvement is needed?
EXAMPLE	I am better prepared at the start of the day	My attendance to registration has improved by 5%	I need to improve my attendance to registration by a further 5%
What did I achieve?			
How do I know I have achieved this? (Evidence)			
It would have been better if …			
I'm happy that I …			
Next time I will …			

Activity

Show Me the Difference

Activity Objective

For the students to demonstrate that there is a measurable progress in aspects of their learning.

Intended Audience

Individual

Spiritual, Moral, Social and Cultural Development Criteria

- Use of imagination and creativity in their learning.
- Willingness to reflect on their experiences.

Context

One of the key questions in mentoring practice is, "How do we know it's working?" ... often disguised as, "I'm not sure if mentoring is working."

This activity is all about the evidence:

- Demonstrating progress
- Enabling the student to be aware of this as progress
- Demonstrating the effectiveness of mentoring

We are ever mindful that students who are working to overcome barriers to learning should not feel that mentoring is now another test to pass or indeed a barrier in itself to overcome. It should be made clear to the student that any assessment carried out within the context of mentoring is essential to monitor their progress, will help them to map their own journey, assist them in providing evidence and ultimately allow them to celebrate their own achievement and progress.

So what methods of assessment, monitoring and evaluation are there? Here's a list to consider:

1. Baseline Assessment
2. Initial Meeting
3. Attendance Registers
4. Databases
5. Mark Books
6. Written Evaluations

7. Oral Evaluations
8. Targets
9. Observations
10. Action Plans
11. Reports
12. Student Records
13. Mentor Meetings
14. One-to-One Interviews
15. Year Team Meetings
16. Comment Books
17. Staff Questionnaire
18. Parental Questionnaire
19. Focus Groups
20. Student Questionnaire

Now we need to work with the students to gather the evidence.

Activity Instructions

1. Look through the grid and consider which of the evidence points you will use to act as a baseline for the beginning of the mentoring intervention.

2. You might want to negotiate the choices here with your student. For example, the student might wish to bring along a sample of work from their English teacher or the result of a Maths test.

3. You might wish to look at the attendance data.

4. Whatever evidence you choose will be the one you use to review and map on the Evidence Grid (Activity Sheet 10).

Closing the Activity

Demonstrating the difference is crucial to all that we do as educators. Ofsted is interested in the impact that interventions have and inspectors want to know:

- How effective have interventions been?
- What are your findings?
- How have you differentiated and personalised your interventions to maximise achievement and attainment for students?

This is an effective activity that clearly demonstrates progress for the student and offers clear focus and direction. This activity gives purpose to mentoring intervention and if a change of direction is needed this activity makes this transparent and clear.

10 Activity Sheet

Evidence Grid

EVIDENCE POINT	DATE	BASELINE FINDINGS	DATE OF REVIEW	REVIEW FINDINGS
Example: Attendance	12/1/2013	84% Attendance	12/5/2013	95%
Example: English Test	1/3/2013	Level 5A	9/10/2013	Level 6C
1				
2				
3				
4				
5				
6				
7				
8				
9				
10				

Activities for Mentoring Young People

Activity

Improving Attendance

Activity Objective
1. To raise student awareness of how attendance at school affects achievement.
2. Students will be able to describe two barriers to their own attendance.
3. Students are to identify two strategies to help improve their own attendance at school.

Intended Audience
Individual or small group setting

Spiritual, Moral, Social and Cultural Development Criteria
- Understanding of the consequences of their actions.
- Willingness to participate in a variety of social settings, cooperating well with others and being able to resolve conflicts effectively.

Context
We know that good attendance has a positive impact upon achievement and we know that poor attendance has an adverse effect. This activity is about raising awareness in this area.

Activity Instructions
1. Read through Activity Sheet 11 'Key Facts About Attendance' and lead a discussion.
2. Give each student a printout of their own attendance data and allow them an opportunity to review/scrutinise it.
3. Brainstorm the reasons for poor school attendance using Activity Sheet 12. Use the brainstorm responses to facilitate a discussion. Key questions to consider:
   - How will your assessment grades/GCSE targets be affected if your attendance does not improve?
   - How will your future plans be affected if your attendance does not improve?
4. Ask each student to select two barriers to good attendance and develop ideas of how to overcome these barriers. Use Activity Sheet 13 to develop strategies for overcoming barriers to good attendance.
5. Finally develop an action plan for improving attendance using Activity Sheet 14. Encourage each student to set specific SMART targets.

Closing the Activity
Consider setting a date to review the 'Improving Attendance Today' Action Plan. Encourage commitment to the plan.

11 Activity Sheet

Key Facts About Attendance

Did you know …?

- By law, all children of compulsory school age (five to 16) must receive a suitable full-time education.

- Parents/carers can receive a fine of up to £2,500, a community order or, in extreme cases, a jail sentence of up to three months if they fail to comply.

- If the court thinks it will help to stop a child missing school, it may also impose a Parenting Order.

- A Parenting Order is a court order which requires parents to attend parenting education or support classes.

(Further information on attendance and updated legislation is available from the Department for Education website www.education.gov.uk)

Activities for Mentoring Young People

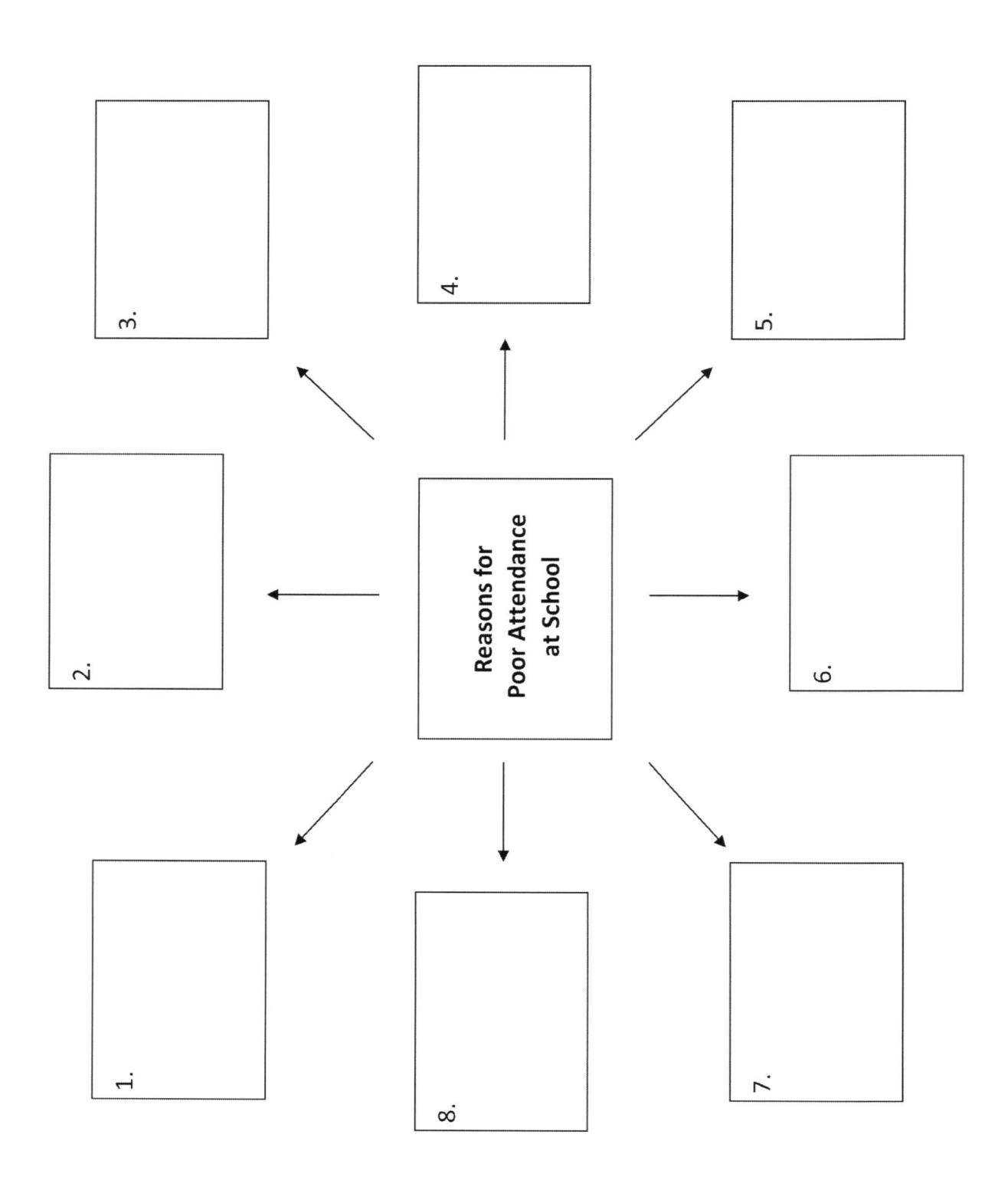

12 Activity Sheet

Reasons for Poor Attendance at School

(Central box: Reasons for Poor Attendance at School, with arrows pointing to eight surrounding boxes numbered 1–8.)

13 Activity Sheet

Overcoming Barriers to Good Attendance

Strategy		
Barrier	1.	2.

Activity Sheet 14

Improving Attendance Today Action Plan

Ensure your plan is **S**pecific, **M**easurable, **A**chievable, **R**ealistic and **T**ime focused (make it SMART).

Aspect	Action/Evidence
a. What can you do to help improve your attendance?	
b. How will you do this?	
c. Who will help you?	
d. How will you know you have been successful?	

Activity

And the Moral of the Story is ...

Activity Objective
The purpose of this activity is to reflect upon the issues of morals by using moral stories. The activity seeks to stimulate the concept of conscience and morality.

Intended Audience
Individual, small group settings or larger classes

Spiritual, Moral, Social and Cultural Development Criteria
- Use of a range of social skills in different contexts, including working and socialising with students from different religious, ethnic and socio-economic backgrounds.
- Ability to recognise the difference between right and wrong and their readiness to apply this understanding in their own lives.
- Understanding of the consequences of their actions.

Context
Students are often faced with dilemmas. The choices can have consequences. An informed individual reduces the risk of finding themselves in a situation of difficulty.

Activity Instructions
1. Read a moral story. A good source is Aesop's fables e.g. 'The Lion and the Mouse' and 'The Two Frogs' (Activity Sheet 15).
2. Brainstorm values and morals (Activity Sheet 16).
3. Students will now create their own moral story.
4. Cut out cards from the 'Story Prompt Sheet' (Activity Sheet 17). Put them face down on the table in three separate piles:
   - One pile for animals
   - One pile for vehicles/transport
   - One pile for location/place
5. The students now create their own moral story and must include the three items selected on their cards.
6. The stories can be shared by being displayed, read at assembly or a school event.
7. The story can be written on the writing frame (Activity Sheet 18).

Closing the Activity
The stories can be written up and shared in the school, displayed or even framed for the students.

A lovely idea is to develop your own book of moral stories for your class, department or school.

Activities for Mentoring Young People

15 Activity Sheet

What is a Moral Story ...?

The Lion and the Mouse

Once when a Lion was asleep a little Mouse began running up and down upon him; this soon wakened the Lion, who placed his huge paw upon him, and opened his big jaws to swallow him. "Pardon, O King," cried the little Mouse: "forgive me this time, I shall never forget it: who knows but what I may be able to do you a turn some of these days?" The Lion was so tickled at the idea of the Mouse being able to help him, that he lifted up his paw and let him go.

Sometime after the Lion was caught in a trap, and the hunters who desired to carry him alive to the King, tied him to a tree while they went in search of a wagon to carry him on. Just then the little Mouse happened to pass by, and seeing the sad plight in which the Lion was, went up to him and soon gnawed away the ropes that bound the King of the Beasts. "Was I not right?" said the little Mouse, very happy to help the lion.

MORAL: Little friends may prove great friends.

The Two Frogs

Two frogs dwelt in the same pool. The pool being dried up under the summer's heat, they left it and set out together for another home. As they went along they chanced to pass a deep well, amply supplied with water, on seeing this, one of the Frogs said to the other: "Let us descend and make our abode in this well." The other replied with greater caution: "But suppose the water should fail us. How can we get out again from so great a depth?"

MORAL: Do nothing without a regard to the consequences (think before you act).

16 Activity Sheet

Ranking Activity

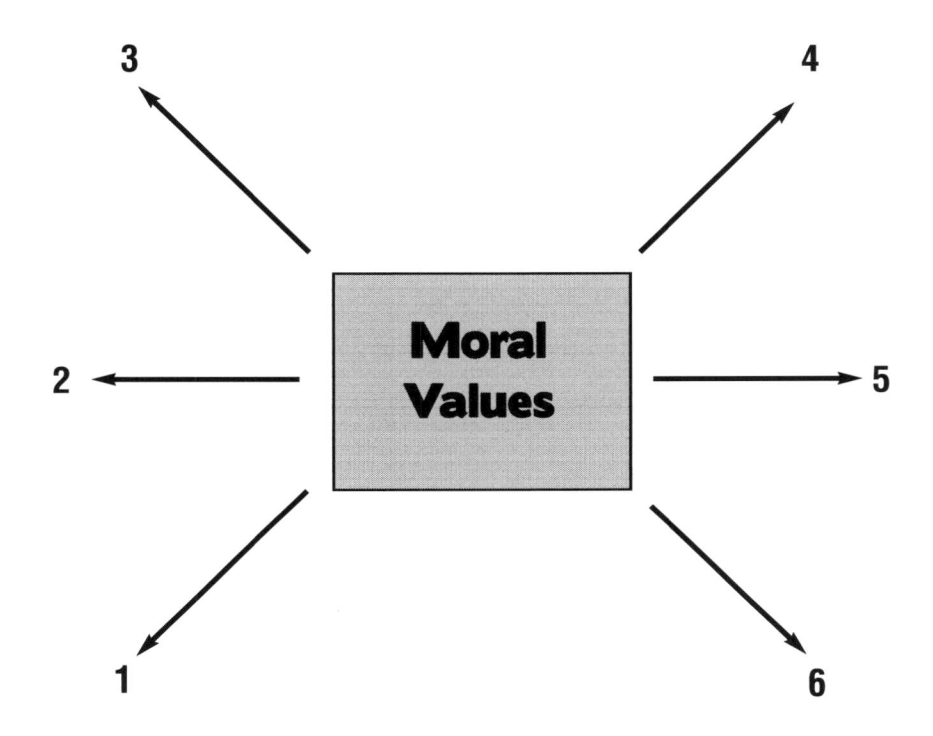

```
        3                           4
         ↖                         ↗
              ┌─────────────┐
    2 ←──────│    Moral    │──────→ 5
              │   Values    │
              └─────────────┘
         ↙                         ↘
        1                           6
```

Now rank these in order of importance to you:

1. _e.g. Trust_____   2. _____

3. _____   4. _____

5. _____   6. _____

17 Activity Sheet

Story Prompt Cards

ANIMALS	VEHICLE/ TRANSPORT	LOCATION/ PLACE
CAT	TRAIN	MANSION
ELEPHANT	BOAT	UNDERGROUND
CROCODILE	PLANE	CASTLE
MOUSE	LORRY	MOUNTAIN
SNAKE	HORSE	ICEBERG
EAGLE	CARRIAGE	DESERT

18 Activity Sheet

Writing Frame

My/our moral story

And the moral of the story is:

Let Me Tell You a Story

Activity Objective
For the students to consider the choices and consequences in the context of a traditional story.

Intended Audience
Individual or small group setting

Spiritual, Moral, Social and Cultural Development Criteria
- Interest in investigating, and offering reasoned views about, moral and ethical issues.
- Understanding the consequences of their actions.

Context
Some students find decision-making difficult. Students may find that a decision made quickly may not yield the desired intention. In this activity students read or listen to a traditional fairy tale. At any point in the story they can stop and advise any character in the story. The idea is to look at what happens when a choice is made and what might happen if a different choice is made.

Here are two examples:

- Cinderella – Cinderella decides that she wants to wear wellington boots to the ball and the fairy godmother grants her wish. What are the consequences for the prince?
- The Three Little Pigs – The pigs decide to build one house, pooling their resources. How does the wolf deal with this? What would happen if the pigs ask the wolf for a loan to fund their project?

Activity Instructions
1. You will need a book of traditional fairy tales. You might want to let a student choose the story.
2. Begin to read the story together. At any time in the story where a decision is being made or a choice is being discussed you can stop and ask the key question, "What would you do?"
3. The next step is to decide what would be the consequences of the student's choice.
4. The Decision-Maker Cards on Activity Sheet 19 can be used to note the decisions and choices made by the student.

5. Key questions (See Activity Sheet 20 – the sheet can be copied and cards cut out so that the students can see the key questions themselves. You can also copy sets of questions if you wish to use this activity with groups):
   - Who would be affected by your choice?
   - What might then happen?
   - In what way has your decision affected the outcome of the story?

Closing the Activity

Draw the activity to a close by asking the students to reflect upon a situation where a choice they have made has affected the outcome.

Ask the students to consider whether a different choice might have led to a more favourable or less favourable outcome.

Activities for Mentoring Young People

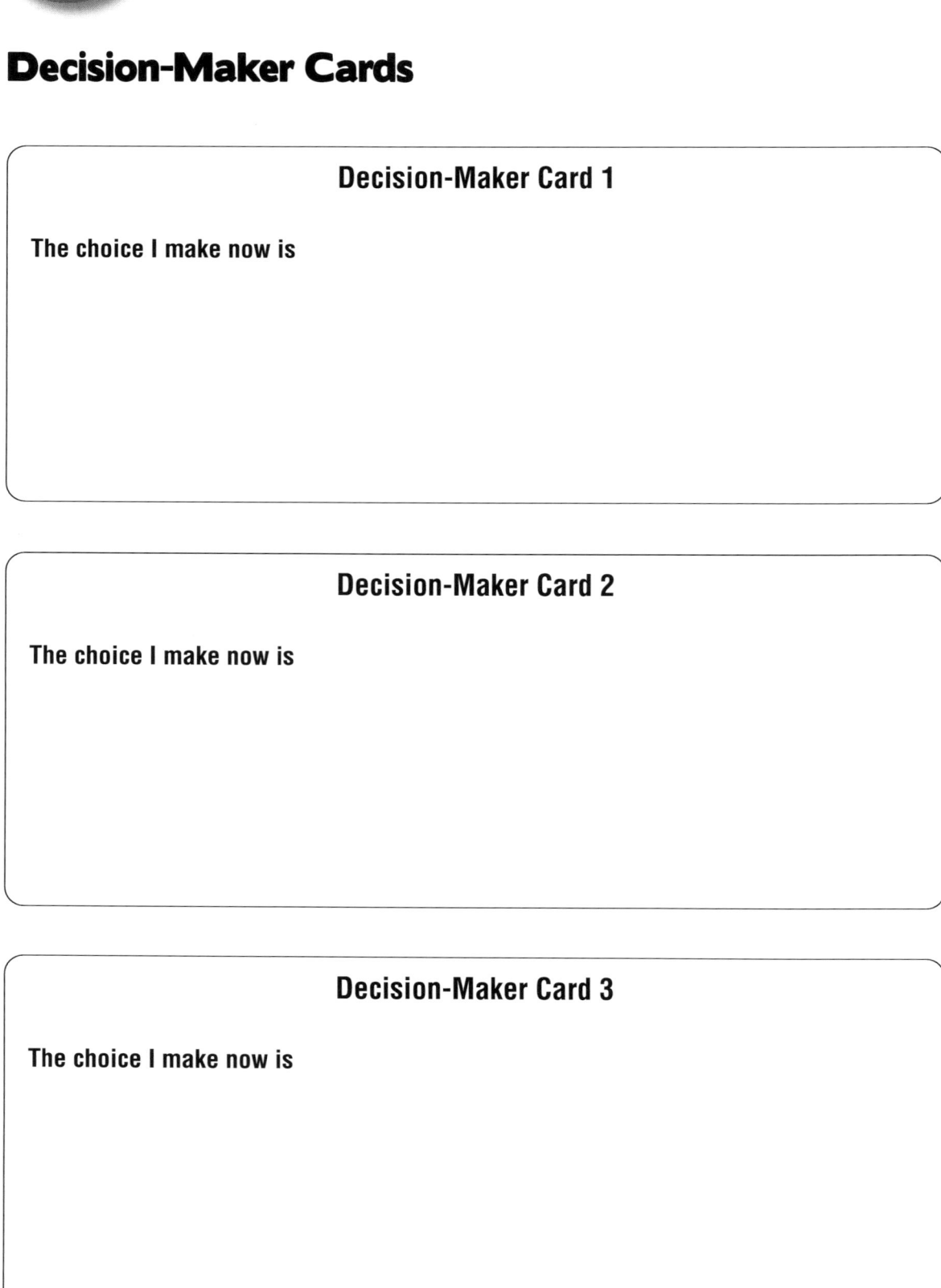

19 Activity Sheet

Decision-Maker Cards

Decision-Maker Card 1

The choice I make now is

Decision-Maker Card 2

The choice I make now is

Decision-Maker Card 3

The choice I make now is

Activity Sheet 20

Key Question Cards

Who would be affected by your choice?

What might now happen?

In what way has your decision affected the outcome of the story?

Activity

What if?

Activity Objective

The purpose of this activity is to help students look at different possibilities and bring a new dimension to issues where the generation of ideas may have stalled. This is a useful activity when students claim there is 'no point' or demonstrate learned helplessness.

Intended Audience

Individual

Spiritual, Moral, Social and Cultural Development Criteria

- Understanding of the consequences of their actions.
- Interest in investigating, and offering reasoned views about, moral and ethical issues.
- Sense of enjoyment and fascination in learning about themselves, others and the world around them, including the intangible.

Context

The 'what if?' scenario is a powerful formative assessment tool to use with a student. When working with the student, you can use the 'What if?' cards in the context of challenging perceptions and developing the 'What if?' scenario with the students.

Activity Instructions

1. Photocopy a few sheets of the cards (Activity Sheet 21), cut them out and have a deck of about 12 cards ready for use.
2. The sample dialogue below illustrates how to use the 'What if?' cards:

Student: There is no point going to college next year, I know I won't get the grades I need.

Mentor: [Turns the 'what if?' card face up]

What if ... you did get the grades that you need?

Student: I might be able to go the college then.

Mentor: What if ... you went to college then?

Student: I might be able to take A Levels.

Mentor: What if you were able to take A Levels?

3. The cards are used to rephrase the student's responses by beginning the sentence with the phrase 'what if' and then writing down the question e.g. "What if you did get the grades?" Seeing the question provides clarity and opens up the possibilities for new thinking.

Closing the Activity

The purpose is to use the 'What if?' cards and phrasing at the beginning of the response to the student and to use the student's own responses to focus the student upon the possibilities of a given situation.

Activities for Mentoring Young People

21 Activity Sheet

What if ...

What if ...

What if ...

What if ...

The Treasure Hunt

Activity Objective

For students to work in a team to make choices; the activity develops problem solving, communication and teamwork skills.

Intended Audience

Small groups or whole class

Spiritual, Moral, Social and Cultural Development Criteria

- Sense of enjoyment and fascination in learning about themselves, others and the world around them, including the intangible.
- Willingness to participate in, and respond to, opportunities in different areas, for example, artistic, musical, sporting, mathematical, technological, scientific and cultural.

Context

The activity aims to develop skills of co-operation, communication, problem solving and teamwork.

Activity Instructions

1. You will need between four and six boxes with lids in which to put different tasks for the students to undertake.
2. Instructions are written and put into each box.
3. Sample tasks for each treasure box are given on Activity Sheets 22-27.
4. Students are provided with a map of where to find the 'boxes of treasure'.
5. Each task is worth 2 points. So if there are six boxes there is a maximum award of 12 points. The aim is to gain maximum points by completing all tasks.
6. Complete the Score Sheet for each group as the students complete the tasks.
7. Once all the activities have been completed, add up the points given for each task completed. The winners are those with the highest number of points.

Closing the Activity

The activity encourages teamwork, co-operation, creativity and decision-making.

The task can be adapted and supplemented or even themed depending upon events in school.

22 Activity Sheet

Treasure Box Task 1

- Inside this box you will find a balloon.

- Blow the balloon up and create a character.

- Show the character to your mentor.

- 2 points for a convincing character.

23 Activity Sheet

Treasure Box Task 2

- Recite your six times table to your mentor.

- It must be correct at the first recitation to earn 2 points.

24 Activity Sheet

Treasure Box Task 3

- There is newspaper and sticky tape in this box.

- Create the tallest free-standing structure that you can and make a paper ball.

- If the structure does not fall down when tested by having the paper ball thrown at it you gain 2 points.

25 Activity Sheet

Treasure Box Task 3

- Create a short scene from the following words:

| SQUIRREL | WITCH | TRAIN |

- Act it out for your mentor.

26 Activity Sheet

Treasure Box Task 5

- There are six straws in this box.

- Create some jewellery or a key ring. You have 5 minutes only.

- Do this in front of your mentor.

27 Activity Sheet

Treasure Box Task 6

- Recite the colours of the rainbow.

OR

- Recite the planets in the solar system.

Sunshine Thinking

Activity Objective

The objective of this activity is to help the students see themselves at their best and in the best light.

Intended Audience

Individual

Spiritual, Moral, Social and Cultural Development Criteria

- Sense of enjoyment and fascination in learning about themselves, others and the world around them, including the intangible.

Context

This activity is called Sunshine Thinking because we want to promote the idea that if all things were 'right and bright' what would the student do?

Activity Instructions

1. Set the scene for the student (Activity Sheet 28).
2. Ask the student the 'Sunshine Questions'.
3. Encourage positive thinking and prompt the student.
4. Having established that there are unlimited possibilities, identify an area to which the student would like to apply 'Sunshine Thinking' and develop some Sunshine Ideas for them using Activity Sheet 29.

Closing the Activity

The activity aims to promote a sense of adventure and offers the opportunity to discuss the possibilities that may not be available to the student when thinking is limited.

28 Activity Sheet

The Sunshine Five

- What would you do if you could not fail?
- If you had all the money you needed, what would you do?
- If you could leave school now, what would you do?
- If you could go anywhere in the world, where would you go?
- If you were leaving university now, what would you do?

Activities for Mentoring Young People

29 Activity Sheet

Sunshine Thinking

I have an issue with _____

_____

_____

If all things were 'right and bright' I would ...

Activity

I Remember When ... It Happened to Me

Activity Objective

To recount a personal story, happiness, episode or experience and reflect upon learning within that personal story.

Intended Audience

Individual or small group setting

Spiritual, Moral, Social and Cultural Development Criteria

- Ability to recognise the difference between right and wrong and students' readiness to apply this understanding in their own lives.
- Use of imagination and creativity in their learning.
- Understanding of consequences of their actions.

Context

This is an activity about reflection and expectation dressed up as an activity about storytelling. Students, adults, little ones, all of us love stories. This activity is about letting a student tell their most interesting stories.

Activity Instructions

1. Ask the students to think back to a poignant experience. Ask them to recount the experience if they wish. They may or may not wish to share the complete story. The important feature of this activity is a guided exploration of the experience.

2. Therein we will find the 'gem' of an experience and that is what we are digging for. Now, using Activity Sheet 30, consider the key questions there.

3. Making a promise: consider asking the students to make a promise to themselves about what they would do if in a similar situation. Use Activity Sheet 31 (The Promissory Note) to enable them to commit and keep this promise to themselves. Ensure they keep it safe.

Closing the Activity

This can be an extremely powerful activity. The experience for the students can act as a pointer for future learning and discovery.

I Remember When ... It Happened to Me

Question 1: What did you learn when that happened?

_____
_____
_____

Question 2: Why do you think this happened?

_____
_____
_____

Question 3: What advice would you give someone else facing the same situation?

_____
_____
_____

Question 4: What would you do differently if you were in this situation again?

_____
_____
_____

Create your own question:

_____
_____
_____

31 Activity Sheet

My Promissory Note

I make this promise to myself …

Activity

Oh No! Sarah's in Trouble

Activity Objective

To create a story looking at issues of conflict and reconciliation.

Intended Audience

Group or pairs

Spiritual, Moral, Social and Cultural Development Criteria

- Interest in investigating, and offering reasoned views about, moral and ethical issues.
- Willingness to participate in a variety of social settings, cooperating well with others and being able to resolve conflicts effectively.

Context

This activity is best used in a pair or with a group of students. It is designed to develop storytelling and creativity. It requires teamwork and problem solving. It aims to help students begin a dialogue by using the language of discord, reconciliation and empathy. The story board is played like a game where the elements of the story are selected. These are then used to write the story.

Activity Instructions

1. Students will need a pair of dice and the Story Board (Activity Sheet 32). The first player throws the dice and moves along the x axis to the appropriate number.
2. The second player throws and moves along up the y axis where the co-ordinates meet.
3. The students select that element as the first in their story. For example: 2 across and 4 up = smile, 'smile' is the first element to be used in the story. All of the elements are recorded on the Story Planning Sheet (Activity Sheet 33).
4. The next player continues and so on until six elements have been selected. The students now have all the elements they need for their story.
5. The next step is to give the students the story title; the suggestion here is 'Oh No! Sarah's in Trouble'. You can differentiate by adapting the title or asking the students to create their own title for their story.
6. The students then create and write up their story using Activity Sheet 34.

Closing the Activity

The story can be shared with the class/group. The story can be displayed or used as a basis for peer assessment.

32 Activity Sheet

Story Board

X \ Y	1	2	3	4	5	6
6	SMILE	LISTEN	MAGIC WAND	SAD	MOUNTAIN	HOUSE
5	WHISPER	WALK	STAR	HAT	TREE	SMILE
4	WALK	SMILE	MOON	LISTEN	STAR	LISTEN
3	LISTEN	TREE	MOUNTAIN	WHISPER	HOUSE	SAD
2	LAUGH	MAGIC WAND	STAR	SORRY	RABBIT	HAT
1	RABBIT	SAD	HOUSE	STAR	WHISPER	SMILE

Activities for Mentoring Young People

Activities for Mentoring Young People

Activity Sheet 33

Story Planning

Dice Throw One

Dice Throw Two

Dice Throw Three

Dice Throw Four

Dice Throw Five

Dice Throw Six

34 Activity Sheet

Our Story: Oh No! Sarah's in Trouble

Activity

Conflict – What it is and How to Deal with it

Activity Objective
To raise awareness of the skills students will need to enable them to mediate between students in conflict.

Intended Audience
Pair, group, individual

Spiritual, Moral, Social and Cultural Development Criteria
- Understanding the consequences of their actions.
- Willingness to participate in a variety of social settings, cooperating well with others and being able to resolve conflicts effectively.

Context
Dealing with conflict appropriately is a life skill. This activity aims to help students develop the skills they need to deal with conflict.

Activity Instructions
1. Ask the students to offer responses to the question, "What is conflict?" Students can jot down their responses or draw on the 'Thought Shower Feedback Cards' (Activity Sheet 35).

2. Students might offer the following responses to the question, "What is conflict?"
   - Disagreement
   - Clash
   - Difference
   - Quarrel
   - Argument
   - Tension
   - Discord
   - War
   - Battle

3. Prompt the students to consider skills and qualities that are needed for successfully dealing with conflict. Hand out Activity Sheet 36 to complete.

4. Students may come up with the following and more:

- Assessment
- Judgement
- Being objective
- Listening skills
- Sharing thoughts
- Choosing
- Ranking
- Justifying
- Debating
- Showing
- Summarising
- Concluding
- Examining
- Selecting

Lead the discussion about which of the qualities your students feel that they have and wish to develop in the future.

5. Now put the learning into practice - ask your students to think of and then describe/relate a situation of conflict, using Activity Sheet 37.

6. Move on to complete the 'Action Plan for Diffusing Conflict' (Activity Sheet 38).

Closing the Activity

These activities give students an opportunity to examine the skills that they already have for dealing with conflict and to plan ways/methods for dealing with situations of conflict.

Review periodically how students are managing situations of conflict. Revisit and adapt the plan as necessary.

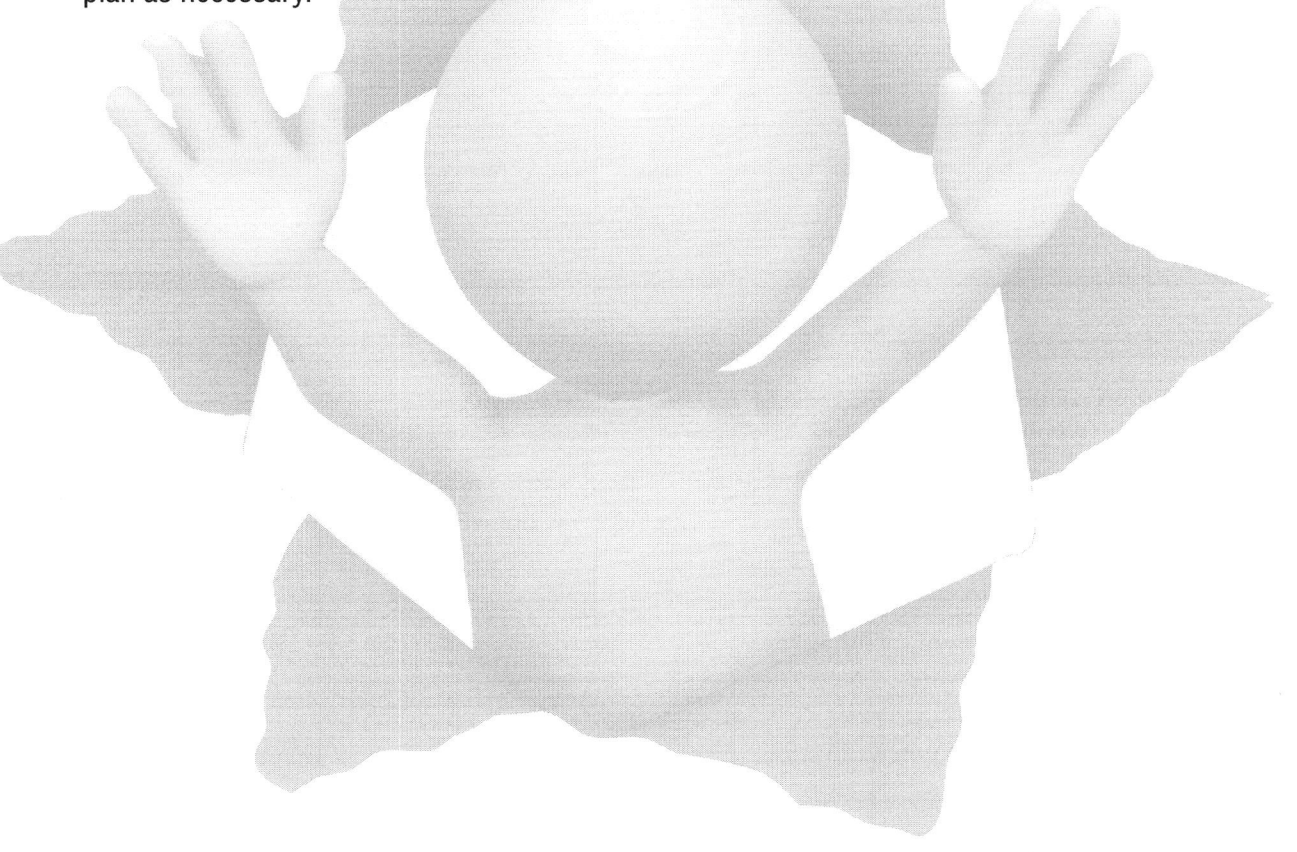

35 Activity Sheet

Thought Shower Feedback Cards

THOUGHT SHOWER FEEDBACK CARD

What is Conflict?

THOUGHT SHOWER FEEDBACK CARD

What is Conflict?

36 Activity Sheet

Resolving Conflict Skills and Qualities

Complete the grid by writing the skills and qualities that you have come up with either on your own, in pairs or in your group.

1.	2.
3.	4.
5.	6.
7.	8.

37 Activity Sheet

A Situation of Conflict

What happened?

Who was affected?

How was the situation resolved?

How could the outcome have been improved?

38 Activity Sheet

Action Plan for Diffusing Conflict

My plans for dealing with conflict

If I am in a situation of potential conflict I will:

a) _____
_____
_____
_____

b) _____
_____
_____
_____

c) _____
_____
_____
_____

Activity

I'm Seeing Red

Activity Objective

For students to recognise the initial signs of anger and identify some ways of diffusing initial anger.

Intended Audience

Individual or small group setting

Spiritual, Moral, Social and Cultural Development Criteria

- Willingness to reflect on their experiences.
- Willingness to participate in a variety of social settings, cooperating well with others and being able to resolve conflicts effectively.

Context

Sometimes students get angry in school and this anger can cause problems in the context of teaching and learning if left to spiral out of control. This activity is about helping students to recognise that they are becoming angry and to then identify some ways of dealing with the anger.

Activity Instructions

1. Ask the students to read/talk through the Why Do I Get Angry? questions (Activity Sheet 39).
2. Ask the students to suggest their own reasons for getting angry. Work through 'What I Do When I'm Angry' (Activity Sheet 40).
3. Lead a discussion on ways of coping and work through 'Coping Strategies' (Activity Sheet 41).
4. Finally students complete the 'Anger Prescription' (Activity Sheet 42) for what they need to do to treat the anger.

Closing the Activity

Review with the students where and when they can get help in a crisis or any given situation.

39 Activity Sheet

Why Do I Get Angry?

1. When I think things are unfair

2. When I'm not being listened to

3. When someone embarrasses me

Now complete some on your own

4. _____

5. _____

6. _____

7. _____

8. _____

9. _____

40 Activity Sheet

What I do When I'm Angry

1. I sometimes shout or use bad language

2. I might hit someone

Now complete some on your own

3. _____

4. _____

5. _____

6. _____

7. _____

8. _____

41 Activity Sheet

Coping Strategies

Generating ways of coping with my anger:

I could _____

I could _____

I could _____

I could _____

I could _____

I could _____

Activity Sheet 42

My Anger Prescription

THREE STEPS:

1. I will _____

_____

_____

2. I will _____

_____

_____

3. I will _____

_____

_____

Activity

Stop Seeing Red

Activity Objective
To identify strategies for coping with highly charged emotional situations following the 'I'm Seeing Red' activity.

Intended Audience
Individual or small group setting

Spiritual, Moral, Social and Cultural Development Criteria
- Willingness to reflect on their experiences.
- Understanding of the consequences of their actions.

Context
Students like TV almost as much as they enjoy the internet and electronic communications. This activity is about using a popular soap character to glean responses to help the students consolidate their learning following the activity 'I'm Seeing Red'. Students will be able to show knowledge of at least four strategies designed to deal with anger.

Activity Instructions
1. Show students a picture of a soap opera character. Choose whatever is popular right now e.g. I have used characters from the BBC's Eastenders with great success. The more volatile or emotive the character, the better.
2. Ask the following:
   - Do students think this character/person has an issue with anger?
   - Students then identify what makes this character angry.
3. Students complete Activity Sheet 43 (Brainstorm).
4. Ask them to consider the social context: friends, family, school/work and environment.
5. Once the students have had the opportunity to generate ideas on the activity sheet, they will be ready to draft a letter of advice to the character.
6. Ask the students to complete Activity Sheet 44, which is a letter of advice to the character.

Closing the Activity
This activity helps the students to consolidate learning developed through the 'I'm Seeing Red' activity and through this one.

Why not post the letter to the producers of the TV show. You never know, you might get a response!

Activities for Mentoring Young People

43 Activity Sheet

Brainstorm

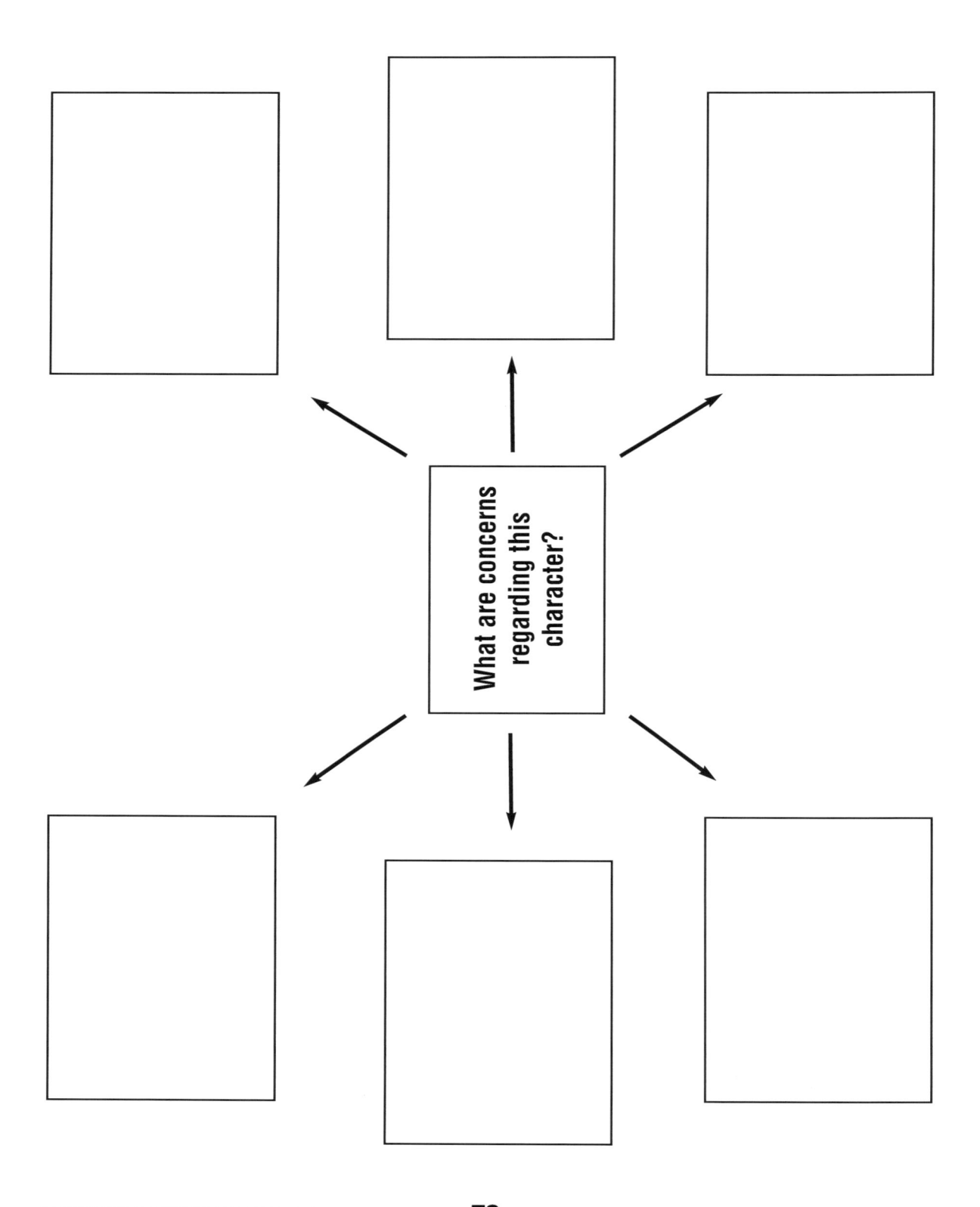

What are concerns regarding this character?

70

© Stephanie George. May be reproduced for instructional use only

44 Activity Sheet

Writing a Formal Letter

Paragraph 1: Explain why you are writing.

Paragraph 2: Add more detail.

Paragraph 3: Write final last sentence, e.g. I look forward to hearing from you.

Signing off: Yours sincerely if you know their name/Yours faithfully if you don't.

Write address here: _____

_____

_____

Write date below: _____

Dear _____

RE: (Character's name) _____

I am writing to let you know that there are many other ways of dealing with anger.

_____
_____
_____
_____
_____
_____

I know it can be hard managing this feeling as

_____
_____
_____

So remember when you get angry

_____
_____
_____

Yours faithfully

Activity

It's About Time

Activity Objective

For students to know how to manage their study time effectively.

Intended Audience

Individual or small group setting

Spiritual, Moral, Social and Cultural Development Criteria

- Use of imagination and creativity in their learning.
- Willingness to reflect on their experiences.
- Sense of enjoyment and fascination in learning about themselves, others and the world around them, including the intangible.

Context

For some students managing time can be a challenge and a barrier to learning and achievement. This activity is designed to help students develop skills to manage their time effectively.

Activity Instructions

1. Ask the students to complete the Time Management Questionnaire (Activity Sheet 45).
2. Read the case study 'Plan Claire's Evening' (Activity Sheet 46) and complete 'Organising Claire' (Activity Sheet 47).
3. Now ask the students to have a go at planning their own time using 'Organising My Time' (Activity Sheet 48). Ask the students to plan their weekday evening.
4. Complete the Review Sheet (Activity Sheet 49).

Closing the Activity

Key questions:

- What did we learn today?
- How does planning our time help with organisation?
- Ask the students to use the plan one evening this week.

45 Activity Sheet

Time Management Questionnaire

Questions:	Response:
Do I use time efficiently? YES/NO (If YES, how?)	
How do I waste time?	
What or who distracts me from my work?	
Do I waste time getting started? YES/NO (If YES, how?)	
Do I find the time passes and I don't know what has happened? YES/NO (If YES, how?)	

46 Activity Sheet

Plan Claire's Evening

- Claire gets home from school at 4:30pm

- Claire has a chapter of a History book to read: 45 minutes

- A Science problem to sort: 30 minutes

- An English assignment: 30 minutes

- Claire wants to ring her boyfriend: 15 minutes

- Watch two programmes at 6:45-7:15pm and 9:30-10:30pm

- Exercise to a video lasting 45 minutes

- By 6pm she will have had her dinner

- Her parents like her to be in bed by 10:30pm

Organise Claire's evening so that she can do all of these things.

47 Activity Sheet

Organising Claire

Use the chart framework to organise Claire's evening

Time	Activity

Activities for Mentoring Young People

48 Activity Sheet

Organising My Time

Use the chart framework to organise your evening. Think about all of the things you need to achieve and create your own plan.

Time	Activity

49 Activity Sheet

Review Sheet

How useful was the plan in helping to manage time?

What issues were encountered using the plan?

What would you change?

Activity

A Place to Study

Activity Objective
To consider the necessary elements for creating a positive environment for successful study.

Intended Audience
Individual or small group setting

Spiritual, Moral, Social and Cultural Development Criteria
- Willingness to reflect on their experiences.
- Use of imagination and creativity in their learning.

Context
As well as good time management, the student needs a purposeful, appropriate and suitable place to study. This activity aims to help students to have ownership and responsibility in organising their own place to study.

Activity Instructions
1. Brainstorm what are the key things needed to create a successful and productive study environment (Activity Sheet 50).
2. Students complete the Study Questionnaire (Activity Sheet 51). The purpose of the questionnaire is to get a picture of the current study environment.
3. Arrange to meet the students after the target day has passed. Complete the Study Questionnaire Review (Activity Sheet 52).

Closing the Activity
Review the plan with the students and discuss its impact upon successful study.

50 Activity Sheet

Brainstorm – My Ideal Study Space

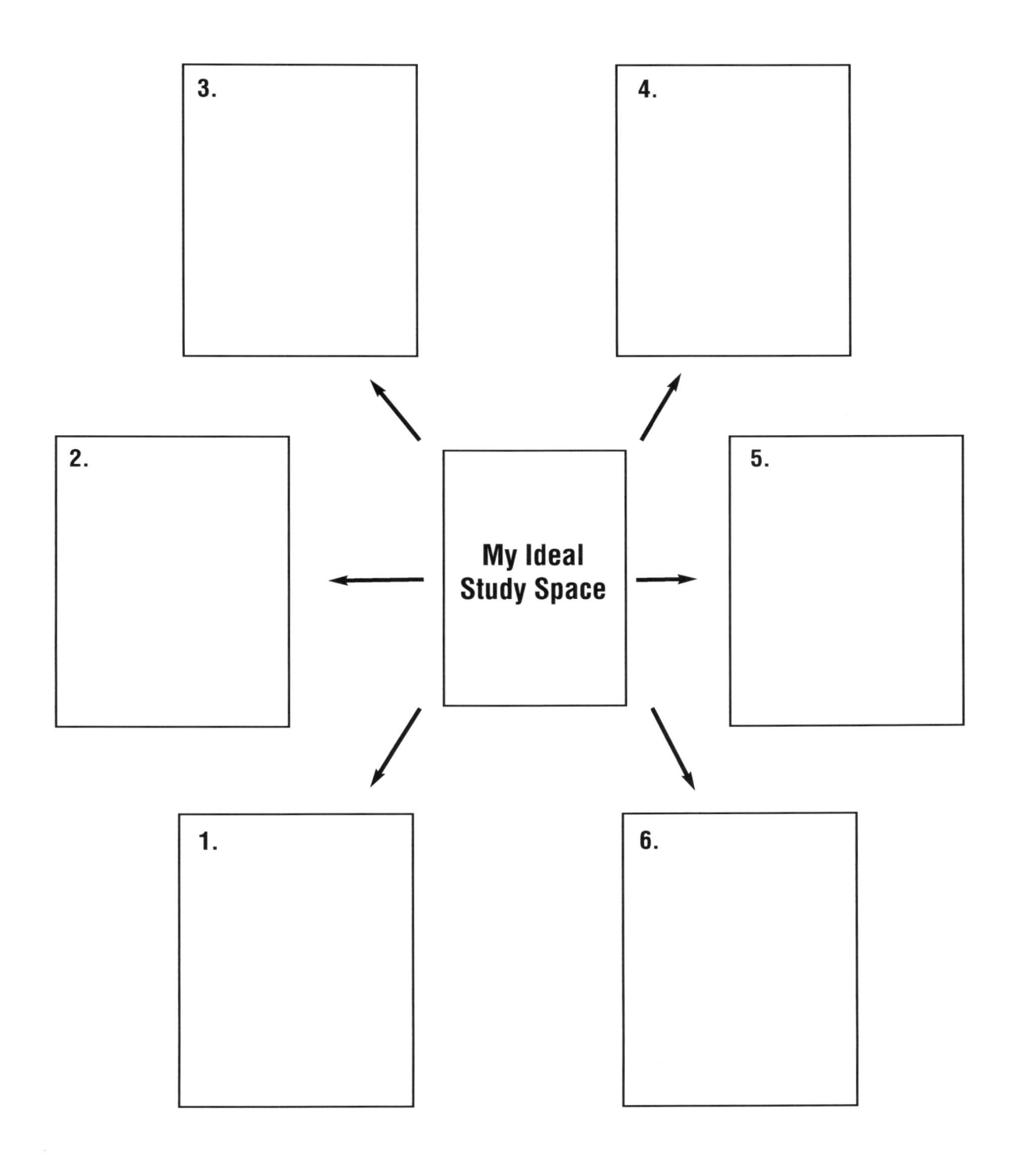

| 3. | 4. |

| 2. | **My Ideal Study Space** | 5. |

| 1. | 6. |

Activities for Mentoring Young People

51 Activity Sheet

Study Questionnaire

QUESTIONS	YES	NO	ACTION NEEDED	REVIEW
I have a suitable space to study at home				
My study space is free of interruption				
I am often disturbed by the telephone or internet				
I have the appropriate writing equipment and stationery for study				
I have the appropriate textbooks and resources				
I know who to ask if I need help with my work				

52 Activity Sheet

Study Questionnaire Review

QUESTIONS	YES	NO	ACTION NEEDED	TARGET DATE	REVIEW
I have a suitable space to study at home					
My study space is free of interruption					
I am often disturbed by the telephone or internet					
I have the appropriate writing equipment and stationery for study					
I have the appropriate textbooks and resources					
I know who to ask if I need help with my work					

© Stephanie George. May be reproduced for instructional use only

Other Useful Resources from Loggerhead Publishing

Conflict Resolution Game CD-Rom

This resource offers a 'fun' way to learn about conflict resolution and is based upon active learning strategies. It helps young people learn about individual and group conflict. The game also addresses issues relating to conflict with adults and those in authority. The 'game board' can be displayed on an interactive whiteboard and is suitable for a class lesson or small groups. Resource cards contain information, facts and issues which help groups and individuals discuss different conflict situations and possible strategies to help resolve them. Topics covered include:

- What is conflict?
- When ideas or views 'clash'
- Avoiding conflict
- Maps of the world
- Understanding others
- Helping others understand you
- Respect
- Empathy
- Being assertive rather that confrontational
- Repairing and rebuilding

Ref 2-124-BK

How to End Lunchtime Troubles CD-Rom

By Dave Stott

Review your current lunchtime systems using this comprehensive assessment and training programme. The resource was developed following requests from schools on how to improve the lunchtime experience for both staff and students. They were concerned about chaotic dining rooms, problem behaviour on the playground, poorly trained and demotivated lunchtime staff and also having to deal with problems which begin during the lunch break and spill over into afternoon lesson time.

- Part 1 – Lunchtime audit. This has a full explanation of how to conduct the audit to establish a 'where are we now' starting point for the programme. The audit is in four main parts requiring input from all key staff. The range of the audit includes information about equipment available, rules, routines and systems, the environment, incidents, activities, health and safety.
- Part 2 – Analysis of the audit information and how to construct an effective action plan.
- Part 3 – Suggested training activities for lunchtime supervisory staff which can act as an induction pack or an ongoing professional development programme.
- Part 4 – Suggested adult-led activities, clubs etc.
- Part 5 – Evaluation.

Ref 035-BK

Peer Counselling CD-Rom

Successfully helps you train students to be peer counsellors. Suitable for students in years 11, 12, and 13, the course can be delivered by teachers or support staff. Focusing on basic counselling and active listening techniques, this CD-Rom can be used to foster emotional health, reduce bullying and improve behaviour in your school.

Ref 2-174-BK

Bullying in Schools DVD

With Ken Rigby

One of the biggest challenges for any teacher is to decide what strategies to use to prevent and resolve bullying at school. This training resource for teachers outlines the pros and cons of six different approaches to bullying. It contains clear and practical guidance and shows how to apply each method, depending on the nature of the bullying and the resources available to deal with it. Whether the bullying involves physical assault, isolation, verbal abuse, or group or one-on-one bullying, this informative DVD will empower you to:

- Build confidence and skills
- Understand more about different options and strategies
- Evaluate which method is likely to be most effective in any given case of bullying.

Using actors and role-play, this DVD is ideal for staff training and teacher training. It helps you make better choices about your approach and shows you how to implement strategies more effectively. The six methods of intervention covered are:

1. The Traditional Disciplinary Approach
2. Restorative Practice
3. Strengthening the Victim
4. Mediation
5. The Support Group Method
6. The Method of Shared Concern

DVD and comprehensive booklet with summary information and useful discussion guidelines. Total running time: 45 minutes.

Ref 019-BK